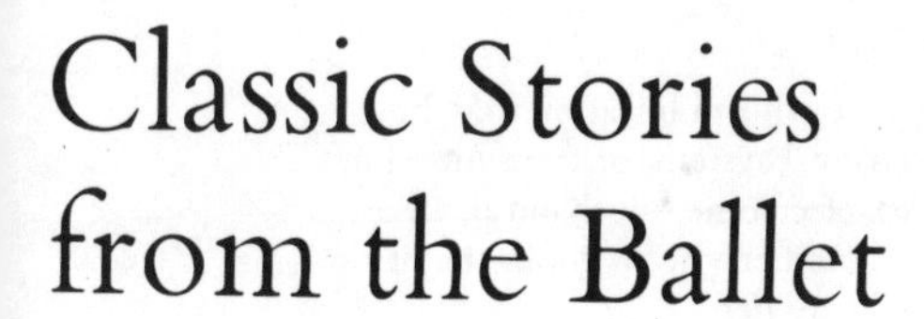

Classic Stories from the Ballet

Retold by Ruth Mindell *and* Jane Reddish

Photographs by Reg Wilson

Longman

1200 word vocabulary

Longman Group Limited
London

Associated companies, branches and representatives
throughout the world

First published 1979

ISBN 0 582 52595 0

We are grateful to the Royal Ballet for permission to reproduce the following copyright photographs of their productions:

Margot Fonteyn in *Swan Lake* on page 4; Merle Park and Anthony Dowell in *Swan Lake* on pages 8–9; the Royal Ballet School in *Coppelia* on page 16; the Royal Ballet School in *Coppelia* on page 21; Antoinette Sibley and Anthony Dowell in *Daphnis and Chloë* on page 25; Antoinette Sibley, Monica Mason and Anthony Dowell in *Daphnis and Chloë* on pages 28 and 29; Vergie Derman and Leslie Edwards in *Sleeping Beauty* on page 36; Antoinette Sibley, Gerd Larsen and Leslie Edwards in *Sleeping Beauty* on pages 40 and 41; Antoinette Sibley, Leslie Edwards and Gerd Larsen in *Sleeping Beauty* on page 44; Keith Rossen, Jennifer Penney and Alexandra Grant in *Petrouchka* on pages 48–49; Merle Park in *Petrouchka* on page 52; Antoinette Sibley and David Wall in *Firebird* on page 57; Rudolf Nureyev in *Nutcracker* on page 60; Merle Park and Rudolf Nureyev in *Nutcracker* on page 65.

The photograph on the cover is from the Royal Ballet production of *Swan Lake*.

We are also grateful to BBC television for permission to reproduce the copyright photograph of Natalia Makarova and Mihail Barishnikov from their production of *Giselle* on page 76.

Contents

Words outside Stage 3 of the New Method Supplementary Readers are in a list on p. 79.

Swan Lake

ACT ONE

It was Prince Siegfried's birthday. He stood with his friends and servants in the palace gardens.

'I thank you for your kindness,' he said to the villagers who had come to wish him happiness.

He took the hand of one of the girls; the village musicians began to play, and everyone danced. Even the prince's old teacher, Wolfgang, joined them. He spun round and round, faster and faster, until his feet left the ground. He fell, just as the queen and her ladies walked down the palace steps. She looked down at him coldly, as the prince helped him to stand up.

'Why were you dancing with the villagers, Siegfried?' she asked.

'Because they have come to wish me happiness.'

'I hope that you will find that happiness tomorrow night,' said the queen, and she looked at everyone with more kindness. 'I have asked the six most beautiful princesses in the world to meet you. One of them must become your wife!'

Siegfried bowed silently.

'But perhaps I won't like any of them!' he said to himself miserably.

'Now you may have your birthday present,' the queen told him, smiling.

A servant stepped forward. He carried a gold crossbow.

'It's beautiful!' Siegfried cried in delight, forgetting all about the princesses.

He kissed the queen's hand, and she returned to the palace. But when the sun had set and the villagers had bowed and left, the prince remembered his mother's words.

'Oh, Wolfgang,' he said sadly, 'how can I marry unless I fall in love?'

'Don't think about that tonight,' replied the old man. 'It's your birthday and you have your new crossbow.'

He picked it up and gave it to the prince. Siegfried pointed it upwards, pretending to shoot the moon. But something else shone in the dark sky.

'Look!' someone shouted. 'Swans! And they're flying towards the lake. Come on!'

ACT TWO

The swans looked like falling stars as they dived over the dark water.

'We'll catch them at the other side,' shouted one of the prince's friends.

They ran on, but Siegfried did not follow them. He sat down by the lake, thinking again of the queen's words.

A line of white swans were sailing along the silver path which the moon made on the waters. The leading swan had a gold crown on its head. When they reached the shore, Siegfried saw them. He jumped up quickly and raised his crossbow. A distant clock struck midnight.

Siegfried stared at the place where the swans had been

'Am I dreaming?' he asked himself.

A crowd of beautiful girls stood on the edge of the lake. They wore dresses of white feathers, and one of them had a gold crown on her head.

'Who are you?' the prince asked wonderingly.

'I am the Princess Odette,' replied the girl with the crown, and her voice was gentle and sad. 'These are my friends,' she said, pointing at the other girls, who all looked at Siegfried with large dark eyes. 'The magician,

Baron Von Rothbart, turned us into swans. When the clock strikes twelve, we turn back into girls. At sunrise, we become swans again.'

'How can you be saved from this evil magic?' cried Siegfried, and his heart beat faster as he looked into Odette's beautiful, sad eyes.

'When someone promises that he will love me for ever and that he is prepared to die for me.'

'I'll promise to love you and to die for you!' the prince shouted. 'I'll tell the world I love you!'

She did not speak, but her eyes shone with love and hope.

He took her hand, and they danced together by the waters of the lake. The other girls danced too. They moved so lightly over the grass that they looked like swans sailing quietly over the water. A silver moon sailed on the water too, and the lake was jewelled with stars.

The shining water darkened as a shadow flew across the moon. A beating of wings crashed through the darkness.

'The magician!' cried Odette, and she and her friends hid their faces in their arms.

A gigantic bird dived out of the sky towards them.

'I'll kill him!' shouted the prince, raising his gold crossbow.

'No!' Odette called, and she moved quickly in front of the bird. 'If he dies before you tell the world you love me, I'll never be free!'

The huge bird stood over them. Its black and green wings waved angrily backwards and forwards, as if they were going to strike Siegfried.

'Don't hurt him!' Odette looked up at the bird. 'Please don't hurt him.'

The bird's eyes shone with evil, but he did not touch the prince. He flew up into a tree, and watched and listened from the branches.

The prince spoke quietly to Odette.

'Tomorrow night at midnight, you must come to the palace. I'll tell everyone of our love, and then you'll be free!'

'There they are! Shoot!' a voice shouted, and Siegfried's friends appeared.

'Stop!' cried Siegfried. 'They're not swans!'

The men stared at the frightened girls, who moved together like a cloud of white feathers. Odette stood in front of them, stretching out her arms to guard them. The men put down their crossbows, and the girls smiled. Four of them began to dance happily like young swans swimming.

Odette and the prince began to dance too, while the stars disappeared one by one.

'We must become swans again,' Odette said sadly, as the moon sailed away, and a red sun lit the sky.

They stepped into the water, and a crowd of white swans swam gracefully away.

ACT THREE

The next evening, the queen sat in her gold chair in the palace. Siegfried stood beside her.

'I wish it were midnight now,' he thought, and he did not hear his mother speaking to him, nor see the six princesses standing in front of him.

'Siegfried!' the queen said again, 'the princesses are waiting to dance with you.'

He stepped forward and bowed to them. The musicians played, and Siegfried danced with each princess. Although they were all beautiful, he hardly saw them.

'When will the clock strike twelve?' he asked himself, and his heart ached for Odette.

He returned to his mother's side.

'Well?' she asked him happily, 'which princess is to be your wife?'

Before he could answer, all the lights in the room went out. When they shone again, two people were standing in front of the prince and his mother. One was a tall man in a black and green cloak; the other was a girl in a dress of black and silver feathers. She looked like a beautiful black swan.

'Odette!' cried Siegfried to himself.

She smiled at him, and his heart felt like a candle thrown into the fire. He did not remember that it was not yet midnight. The queen asked the strangers to sit beside her.

'Let the dancing begin,' she commanded.

Dancers from all over the world spun in front of the prince's eyes, but he did not see them; the music played, but he did not hear it. All he saw were the dark shining eyes and the black and silver feathers of the girl beside him; all he heard was the beating of his heart.

He did not know that the tall man in the dark cloak was Baron Von Rothbart, and that the girl was his daughter, Odile. The magician had used his evil powers to make her look exactly like Odette.

The dancers left, and the musicians began to play again.

Baron Von Rothbart spoke quietly in Odile's ear: 'Make him tell everyone that you are the princess he loves!'

She laughed and moved closer to Siegfried.

They danced, and she was so light and moved so quickly that she seemed to fly out of his arms, and he could not hold her. Then she looked back at him, smiling, and he followed her, wanting her more and more.

Outside, a white swan beat its wings helplessly against the window. Odile heard the sound. She looked up and saw the bird. Quickly, she moved into the prince's arms and danced with him to the other end of the room.

The white swan's eyes filled with tears. They fell one by one on to its white feathers. But Siegfried had his arms round Odile and was saying to her, 'I love you, I love you.'

He brought her to the queen. He bowed and said, 'I wish this princess to be my wife. I promise that I'll love her, and only her, for ever.'

'You fool!' laughed Odile, and the room went dark. A wild wind blew the tall man's black and green cloak backwards and forwards like the wings of a huge bird. Siegfried cried out in fear. Then he heard wings beating against the window. He looked up and saw the white swan, and he knew what he had done.

'Odette, Odette! Forgive me!'

He ran from the palace as the clock struck twelve.

ACT FOUR

Odette stood by the lake, her tears still falling.

'I shall kill myself!' she cried, but her friends pulled her away from the cold, dark water.

'Odette! Odette!' she heard Siegfried's voice calling, as he ran towards the lake.

The magician tried to stop him.

'Blow him back!' he called to the wind. 'Catch him in your branches!' he cried to the trees.

Siegfried fought against the wind; he pushed the waving branches aside; at last, he stood in front of Odette. She covered her face with her hands and turned away.

'You have broken my heart,' she said. 'You told Odile you loved her.'

'But I thought she was you!' he told her. 'Can you ever forgive me?'

She kissed him sadly. They danced by the edge of the lake, as they had done the night before. But this time, their dancing was full of sorrow, because Odette could never be free.

'I can't leave you,' she said to Siegfried, as the moon disappeared in the pale sky.

As she spoke, a huge bird flew down. It forced Odette towards the lake, but Siegfried struck at it with his hands. It beat at him with its powerful wings, but the prince would not let it reach Odette. It flew to the edge of the lake and waved its black and green wings over the water. A gigantic dark wave rolled over the shore towards them. Siegfried seized Odette and carried her safely to the top of a high rock.

'I don't want to live without you,' she told him.

'Let's die together!' he cried.

Hand in hand, they jumped into the deep lake. The waters closed over them. The magician gave a fearful cry, and the huge bird fell to the ground dead. The evil power had been destroyed because Siegfried had given his life for Odette.

A golden boat, pulled by white swans, sailed across the quiet lake. It carried the spirits of Siegfried and Odette to a heaven where their love would live for ever.

Coppelia

ACT ONE

Doctor Coppelius lived in a small town in Galicia. He made wonderful dolls which looked like real people; they moved their arms and legs by clockwork. But Doctor Coppelius wanted them to move without clockwork; he wanted them to become living people, who could breathe and talk and dance. He studied old books of magic, hoping to find a spell which could give his dolls life.

His favourite doll had bright blue eyes and pale golden hair. He called her Coppelia, and he told everyone that she was his daughter. He put her in a chair by the window above his shop; she looked as if she were reading a book. Everyone who walked along the street could see her.

Swanilda lived on the other side of the street. She was in love with a man called Franz, who loved her too. Everyone expected them to marry in the spring. But since Coppelia had appeared, Franz seemed to have forgotten Swanilda. Every day, he stood in front of Doctor Coppelius's shop, staring up at the beautiful doll. He thought she was a real girl.

'I wish she would smile at me. Then I'd tell her I love her,' he thought, but she never looked up from her book.

His love for Coppelia made Swanilda both sad and angry.

'I don't believe that she is real,' she said to herself, 'but I must find out.'

One day, when the street was empty, she ran over to

the shop, and looked up at the window.

'Coppelia!' she called. 'Coppelia, please speak to me!'

Coppelia said nothing; she did not move her eyes away from her book.

'Perhaps if I dance,' thought Swanilda, 'she'll look up.'

As she danced in front of the shop, she looked again and again at the window, but Coppelia did not seem to notice her.

'She's only a doll!' Swanilda decided, 'but how can I make Franz believe that?'

She walked slowly back to her house. She did not see Franz at the other end of the street.

He hurried to the shop, and stared up at the beautiful doll.

'I wish she would look at me,' he told the empty street. Behind the curtains of the window, Doctor Coppelius stood watching Franz. He heard his words, and he smiled to himself. He turned the clockwork key in Coppelia's back. Slowly, she stood up, still holding the book in her hand. She began to dance. Franz's heart beat fast.

'I wish I could dance with her!' he thought, as he smiled up at her.

The clockwork slowed down. Coppelia stood still. Doctor Coppelius took her by the arm and carried her away from the window. Franz walked down the street, and his heart sang with happiness.

At the end of the day, when all the people of the town had finished their work, they gathered in the street to talk. Swanilda joined them, and soon they began to dance and sing.

'Quiet, everyone, please be quiet!' called a loud voice. It was the Burgomaster.

'Tomorrow is to be a holiday! The Duke of Galicia is

irsch"

coming to our town. He is going to give us a new bell. And,' he added, smiling at everyone, 'he'll give a handful of gold coins to any girl who receives a promise of marriage during the holiday!'

The Burgomaster turned to Swanilda, who was standing next to him.

'Will you be one of them?' he asked her.

Swanilda only smiled at him sadly.

As the Burgomaster left, the singing and dancing began again. Soon the sun disappeared over the roofs of the houses and the lamps were lit.

'Good night!' the people of the town called to each other. 'Good night!'

When the street was empty, Doctor Coppelius came out of his shop for his evening walk. Carefully, he locked the door with a heavy iron key, and put it away in his coat. As he turned to go, a group of young men appeared and danced round him.

'Join our dance!' they shouted and laughed at him.

They took him by the arms and spun him around. He nearly fell, and his key dropped to the ground. No one noticed it.

'Leave me alone!' he cried angrily.

They laughed, and left him. He pulled his hat down over his head, picked up his walking stick, and went up the street. He was very angry.

It was a warm night; no one wanted to sleep. Swanilda and her friends stood in the street talking about the holiday.

'I hope I shall have a handful of gold coins tomorrow!" one of them said.

'Will Franz ask you to marry him tomorrow?' another asked Swanilda.

'He's in love with Coppelia,' she replied, and looked sadly at the shop across the street. She saw something shining on the ground in the light of the lamp.

'It's a key!' she cried.

They all ran across the street, and Swanilda picked up the key.

'It's Doctor Coppelius's key!' she said, and she looked at the locked door. 'Shall we go into his house?'

'Oh, yes! Let's go in. I've always wanted to see his dolls!' one of the girls cried.

Softly, Swanilda turned the key in the lock. They stepped into the darkness, feeling a little frightened. Swanilda lit a lamp, and they all walked quietly up the stairs.

Franz, too, had not gone to bed.

'Tonight, I'm going to speak to Coppelia,' he decided.

He carried a ladder over to the shop, and placed it against the top window. He began to climb.

'What are you doing?' shouted an angry voice.

Doctor Coppelius had returned from his walk and stood at the foot of the ladder, looking up at Franz. Franz jumped down and ran quickly up the street.

'Come back!' cried Doctor Coppelius, and he waved his walking stick at him. He ran after him as fast as he could, but Franz was too quick for the old man.

While Doctor Coppelius was still looking for him at the other end of the street, Franz ran quietly behind the houses until he reached the shop again. He began to climb the ladder.

ACT TWO

Inside, the girls had found a house full of people.

'Who are they?' they asked each other quietly. 'Why don't they speak to us? Why don't they move?'

Then one of the girls laughed. 'They're only dolls! Look, this one has a key in its back. Perhaps, if I turn the key, the doll will move.'

The girls were delighted when it started to dance. They looked at the other dolls and found that they all had keys. Soon, the whole room was full of dancing dolls. The girls danced with them, pretending that they were dolls too.

Swanilda noticed a curtain at the end of the room. She was curious to know what was behind it. She drew it back—and looked into the beautiful blue eyes of Coppelia.

'I hope I didn't frighten you,' she said to her, thinking for a minute that she was a real person. Coppelia did not reply. Swanilda touched her arm gently, and she fell to one side.

'Now I know you're only a doll!'

As she stood looking at Coppelia, she heard a noise. She looked round the curtain, and saw Franz climbing into the room.

'I'll play a game with him!' she said to herself. 'I'll pretend to be Coppelia!'

She changed into the doll's clothes, and pushed the doll into a dark corner. But, before she could step out into the room, Doctor Coppelius appeared at the top of the stairs.

'Get out of my house!' he was shouting, as he waved his stick at the frightened girls.

They ran out of the room and down the stairs and out into the street.

Doctor Coppelius came in and saw Franz, who was still standing by the window.

'How dare you come into my house!' he shouted at him.

Franz threw himself in front of him.

'Please forgive me!' he cried. 'I love your daughter! I want to ask her to marry me.'

'So, you want to marry my daughter?' said the old

man, smiling happily and pushing Franz into a chair.

'We'll have to think about that! But, first of all, we'll have a drink together.'

As he hurried off to find two glasses, he said to himself, 'I'll use his soul to give life to Coppelia! I'll make him sleep, and then I'll look for a spell.'

He dropped a sleeping powder into the drink and gave the glass to Franz. Franz drank it all. The glass dropped from his hand. He was asleep. Doctor Coppelius sat down with an old book of magic. He began to read out a strange spell in a loud voice, and to touch Franz's closed eyes with his fingers. As he finished reading the spell, the curtain at the end of the room opened. Swanilda, dressed in Coppelia's clothes, stepped out.

'It's worked! The spell's worked!' the old man shouted, jumping up and down in excitement.

Swanilda walked towards him, moving her arms and legs slowly like a doll. But then she began to move quickly, until she was dancing round the room like a real girl. Doctor Coppelius was delighted, but he stopped smiling at her when she began to tear the pages out of his book of magic.

'Stop it!' he shouted at her, but she danced away from him. She threw the other dolls on the floor and tore their clothes.

'Oh! What have I done?' cried the old man helplessly. 'How can I stop her? Perhaps, if I give her a present, she'll leave the dolls alone.'

He found a bright red Spanish shawl, and threw it over her. She smiled at him and began to dance. Stormy Spanish music filled the room, and Doctor Coppelius seemed to feel the burning sun and the hot, dry dust of Spain. When the dance was finished, he gave Swanilda a Scottish plaid. She danced again, with her arms held

high. Her feet moved backwards and forwards so quickly that it looked as if she were dancing over sharp swords. Doctor Coppelius thought he could hear the strange, wild sound of Scottish pipes.

The sound of the dancing woke Franz.

'Coppelia!' he cried, running towards Swanilda.

She moved quickly back to the end of the room and pulled back the curtain. Franz looked at the doll with the beautiful blue eyes and pale golden hair lying on the floor. Then he looked at the living girl standing at his side.

'Oh, Swanilda!' he said, 'Can you ever forgive me for falling in love with a doll, and forgetting you?'

Swanilda kissed him.

'I was going to ask Coppelia to dance with me,' he told her, 'and then I was going to ask her to marry me!'

They both laughed, and began to dance among the dolls which lay on the floor. They had forgotten about Doctor Coppelius. He watched them as they danced down the stairs and out of his shop. He looked at Coppelia lying in the corner. He threw himself down on the floor beside his dolls and the torn pages of his book of magic, and he wept.

ACT THREE

The next morning, everyone gathered in the town to see the duke. Doctor Coppelius hurried outside, as soon as the duke arrived, and bowed to him.

'She's spoilt my wonderful dolls, my lord,' he said, pointing at Swanilda. 'She must be punished.'

'Please don't punish her, my lord!' cried Franz, stepping forward. 'She's very sorry. She spoilt the dolls because I was in love with one of them! But now I've asked her to marry me.'

The duke laughed, and gave Swanilda a handful of gold coins.

'And a bag of gold for Doctor Coppelius!' he said, putting it into the old man's hand. 'Now, let the new bell ring to bless us all!'

Swanilda and Franz stood hand in hand listening to the bell, as it rang joyfully through the town. Its music made everyone want to dance and sing, and even Doctor Coppelius smiled, as he walked back to his shop.

Daphnis and Chloë

Scene One

The dark blue sea rolled quietly backwards and forwards over the white sands. The rocks shone red in the evening light. Deep in a cave sat the great god Pan. He played his pipes and the nymphs of Pan sang a strange song to the music.

They stopped singing when they heard the noise of talking outside their cave. The villagers, who looked after the sheep on the mountain, had come down to the shore with presents of fruit and flowers for their god. They had never seen Pan nor heard his music, but they knew that he lived in the cave.

They placed the shining fruit and bright red and golden-yellow flowers at the foot of the rock which guarded the entrance. Then they solemnly danced in honour of Pan and his nymphs. The sun went down slowly over the sea, and, one after the other, the villagers sat down to rest, until only two dancers were left. Their shadows grew long and seemed to dance by themselves right into Pan's cave.

The god saw them and said to his nymphs, 'Those are the shadows of Daphnis and Chloë, who love each other, and who love us.'

Outside the cave, the villagers watched the two dancing together.

One of the girls said, 'Let's make Daphnis dance with us!'

The others laughed and jumped up quickly.

They surrounded him, crying, 'Dance with us, Daphnis, dance with us!'

They held his hands; he smiled, and they began to dance.

Chloë gave him a quick, unhappy look, and turned away. She felt alone and sad, as if he had left her for ever. But the other men called to her, 'Chloë, dance with us!' She walked slowly towards them. They moved in a circle around her, all laughing happily. She looked up and smiled. Then she too began to dance.

Suddenly, one of the men seized her hand roughly and kissed her.

'Go away!' she cried angrily, trying to free herself.

'Dorkon! Leave her alone!' shouted Daphnis, as he pushed his way through the dancers.

Everyone stood back, a little afraid, as Daphnis and Dorkon faced each other in angry silence. They both raised an arm.

'They're going to fight!' cried one of the girls. 'Stop them!'

A man stepped forward quickly.

'Don't fight,' he said. 'Instead, let's see who is the best dancer. The one who wins can have a kiss from Chloë!'

This pleased everyone, and they sat down to watch. First, it was Dorkon's turn. His movements were heavy and ungraceful. He tried to jump through the air like the great god Pan himself, and almost fell. Everyone laughed at him. He hated them all, and most of all he hated Daphnis.

Daphnis smiled at Chloë and began his dance. Pan's nymphs looked from their cave.

'He dances like a god,' they said to one another.

He was strong and could spring high into the air. He was graceful and could move as lightly as the gently-waving flowers which grew among the rocks.

'Well done! Well done!' Everyone crowded round him, shaking his hand, and shouting, 'Daphnis has won!'

'And now my kiss!' he laughed.

Chloë ran to him and kissed him.

He put his arms round her, while she said softly in his ear, 'Oh, Daphnis, I love you!'

'It's time to bring the sheep down for the night,' someone called.

The sun had disappeared and large stars shone in the dark sky. They all prepared to leave the sea shore and return to the mountain, where their sheep wandered among the grass and rocks. But Daphnis stood in front of the cave, still hearing in his ear Chloë's words of love, and feeling her soft kiss.

He heard a step behind him. Cool hands covered his eyes.

'Chloë! Chloë, my love!' he said, pulling the hands away from his face, and turning round.

But it was not Chloë who stood there smiling at him. It was Lykanion. She was a young woman who had once lived in the village, but had gone to the town where she had married a rich, old man.

'Are you pleased to see me again?' she asked.

He looked at her and thought, 'How lovely she is!'

'Well, are you pleased?' she said again.

'Oh, yes!' he replied, and he could think of nothing else to say.

The way she looked at him with her dark shining eyes frightened him.

'Dance with me,' she said.

She raised her white arms above her head and moved slowly round him. Her red dress shone like fire in the starlight, and her beauty seemed to burn him. He knew that he should go to help Chloë with the sheep; he knew that he should not stay with Lykanion; but he could not leave her.

They danced together over the sand and among the rocks. Daphnis became more and more excited by her beauty. He seized her in his arms and was just going to kiss her, when the air was filled with rough shouts. A crowd of men appeared. Each held a lamp in one hand and a sharp, pointed knife in the other.

'Pirates!' cried Lykanion, and she ran quickly away behind the rocks.

'Chloë! I must find Chloë!' thought Daphnis, but as he ran forward, he heard her frightened voice.

She was calling his name and running towards him. Two pirates were behind her and they seized her. As Daphnis threw himself towards them, Dorkon sprang out from behind a rock with a knife in his hand.

'Get back!' he shouted at Daphnis.

'Take her to your king,' he told the men, pointing at Chloë.

They carried her away, and Dorkon laughed.

'Now the pirates can have her kisses!' he called to Daphnis, as he disappeared into the darkness.

Daphnis stood alone in the silence outside Pan's cave.

He put his hand to his head, and cried out in helpless misery, 'What can I do? What can I do?'

Inside the cave, Pan's nymphs heard him calling.

'The man who dances like a god needs our help,' they told one another.

Quickly, three of the nymphs ran from the cave and stood in front of him.

'Your love will be found,' they sang to him in their strange voices. 'The great god Pan has heard your cries.'

Scene Two

Chloë shook with fear, as the pirates carried her to their king.

'We have a present for you from the villagers,' they laughed.

They laid her on the ground in front of him. King Bryaxis stood over Chloë and smiled, and his smile was evil.

'Lie there and see how my pirates dance,' he said. 'But first, we will tie your hands, so that you can't escape.'

With her hands tied together, Chloë stared miserably at the pirates, who stood in front of a huge fire.

'Dance!' commanded their king.

They raised their arms to the sky, threw back their heads, and began to move. They danced slowly at first; then faster and faster. Their dark eyes shone, and their brown fingers seemed to command the world to watch them. They wore clothes of red and black, with gold rings in their ears, and gold circles around their arms and about their necks. They shone in the darkness like the fire. They shouted with excitement as they spun across the grass, until at last they stopped in front of Bryaxis.

'Now you will dance with me,' he said to Chloë, and he pulled her to her feet.

She was so frightened that she could hardly stand. The rope around her hands bit into her skin. But the music which the pirates made with their strange instruments suddenly filled her with excitement. She freed herself from the king, and danced in the light of the fire.

'You dance well,' said the king, as the music ended, and Chloë stood in front of him.

He put his arms round her, and she tried to fight him off. He kissed her, and she turned her face away.

'Come now,' he said angrily, 'you're mine!'

'No! Never!' she said proudly, and he raised his hand to hit her.

'Do not strike her!' called a voice, and the sound of pipes sounded through the air.

A strange light shone about them. Chloë stepped back and the ropes fell from her hands.
'I'm free!' she cried in wonder.
The light was becoming brighter. The air was full of softly singing voices.
'It's Pan!' shouted Bryaxis, as the strange form of the god came slowly towards him.
The pirate king gave a great cry of fear, and ran away into the darkness.

Scene Three
Daphnis had searched all night for Chloë, but Pan's nymphs had used their magic powers to keep him away from the pirates, who would have killed him. As the night ended, Daphnis found himself standing on the sea shore. He was too tired to go any further. He lay down on the sand and fell asleep.

The sun rose and warmed the cold sand. The sea birds flew over his head singing joyfully. Voices called along the shore: 'Daphnis, Daphnis! Where are you?'
His friends were looking for him. One of them was playing a pipe, and his music joined the songs of the birds.
'There he is!' someone shouted.
They ran forward and knelt beside him on the sand.
'Wake up, wake up!' they laughed.
He stretched, and opened his eyes to the bright sun and their happy faces.
'The pirates have gone!' they told him.
'Chloë! Where's Chloë?' he cried, and jumped up quickly.
'I'm here!' Chloë threw herself into his arms. 'Pan saved me!'
'Oh, Pan! Oh, wonderful Pan! We must give thanks

to him,' said Daphnis, as he kissed her, 'and we must ask him to bless our love.'

They all danced along the shining sand until they reached the god's cave. They stood in silence and bowed.

Daphnis took Chloë's hand and said solemnly, 'Oh, great god Pan, we thank you for coming to help us, and we ask your blessing on our love.'

The cave was full of light and music.

'He has answered!' cried Chloë. 'Pan has blessed us!'

Everyone began to dance, laughing and singing in joy and wonder. They spun, they jumped, they moved to and fro among the rocks and over the sand. Pan played his pipes louder and louder; the nymphs sang more and more joyfully, and the sun itself seemed to dance in the sky.

The Sleeping Beauty

Once upon a time in a magic land lived a king and his beautiful queen. They loved each other very much, but one thing spoilt their happiness: they did not have a child.

One summer day, the queen was sitting by the lake in the palace gardens. A frog jumped up on to the path at her feet and spoke to her.

'Madam, I know that your greatest wish is to have a child. Soon you will have a daughter!'

Before the queen could question him, he dived back into the water. The queen ran to the palace and told the king what the frog had said. The baby was born in the spring, and they named her Aurora.

'We must ask all our people to see their new princess, and we will ask the seven fairies to come and bless her,' they decided.

The first scene

All the visitors were met by the Lord Chamberlain at the entrance to the great hall of the palace. They bowed to the king and queen. The Princess Aurora was carried in and placed in a little bed beside her mother's gold chair.

One after the other, the seven fairies appeared in front of the king and queen. Each one danced. The great hall was full of soft, moving colours. The only sound was the gentle noise of lightly-waving wings.

Each of the fairies walked over to the baby princess's bed. They held their silver wands over her, while they gave their blessings:

'The Princess Aurora will be beautiful.'

'She will be good.'

'She will be graceful.'

'Aurora will sing like a bird.'

'The Princess will be kind.'

'She will be wise.'

'She will be . . .' but the seventh fairy's blessing was never finished.

A loud crash shook the hall, and a dark cloud hung in the air.

'What's happening? Why is it so dark?' frightened voices cried.

The cloud cleared. A strange old woman, in a dusty black cloak which shone with green dots of light, stood in front of the king and queen.

'Why didn't you ask me to come and bless your daughter?' she asked them, and her voice was hard and angry. 'I am the fairy Carabosse!'

'You must be the fairy who left our land many years ago,' said the king.

His face was pale when he remembered the stories of her evil powers. 'We are sorry that we did not ask you to come,' he added, as he looked into her cold green eyes.

'It's too late to be sorry!' she cried. 'You didn't ask me. I have come to give your daughter my blessing.'

She lifted her thin hand over the baby's head, and said in a loud voice, 'The Princess Aurora will cut her finger on a spindle and die!'

The queen cried out as if she had been struck through the heart with a sword, 'Oh, my beautiful baby'.

Carabosse's evil laugh rang through the great hall. A soft sound of wings made her stop. Turning round, she saw the seventh fairy.

'The Lilac Fairy!' she cried. She was angry and afraid, because she knew that the fairy's magic powers were as strong as her own.

'I have not yet given my blessing to the Princess Aurora,' said the Lilac Fairy, 'but I will bless her now.'

Holding her silver wand over the sleeping child, she said, 'I can't change that evil spell completely, but Aurora shall not die. Instead, she will sleep for a hundred years. A prince's kiss will wake her.'

'How dare you change my spell!' shouted Carabosse.

She pulled her cloak around her, and disappeared in a dark cloud.

'To sleep for a hundred years!' cried the queen sadly.

She held the baby's small fingers in her long white hand, and her tears fell on the child's peaceful face.

'She must never touch a spindle!' she said.

The king stood in the centre of the hall, and spoke in a loud voice, so that everyone should hear his words.

'All spindles must be destroyed! My soldiers will search every corner of the land. If they find that anyone has hidden a spindle, he will die!'

ACT ONE

Aurora grew up as beautiful and as good as the fairies had promised. When she was sixteen, her father and mother decided to have a dance for her birthday. They asked all the important people of their land, and four rich princes from countries far away over the sea. Each of the four princes hoped that the beautiful Princess Aurora would fall in love with him.

The palace was full of joy and excitement. A hundred baskets of flowers hung in the great hall. The soft light from a thousand candles filled the room. The king and queen sat on their gold chairs. The jewels in their crowns shone like coloured stars.

The Lord Chamberlain bowed to them.

'The dancers from the villages!' he said loudly, and

into the hall came a crowd of excited villagers.

They looked so happy and so proud as they danced for their king and queen, that all the important visitors were delighted.

'The Princess Aurora!' called the Lord Chamberlain.

As she walked in, everyone stood up to look at her. She was wearing a dress which was the colour of a wild rose, and it shone with jewels like bright drops of early morning water in a flower.

Aurora danced for her mother and father, and their eyes were bright with happiness as they watched their beautiful daughter.

When the music stopped, she stood quietly beside her mother. The four princes were led into the great hall.

'We are pleased that you have come to join us on our daughter's birthday,' said the king solemnly.

The princes bowed to him, and then to the queen, who stepped forward and touched the hand of each prince in turn.

'You may dance with the Princess Aurora,' she told them, smiling happily at her daughter.

Each prince gave Aurora a rose to tell her that he loved her, but she only smiled and gave the flowers to the queen. She danced with each prince.

The people in the great hall smiled and said to one another, 'She's as graceful as the third fairy promised sixteen years ago.'

No one could look anywhere but at the lovely princess. No one noticed an old woman in a black cloak standing in the corner. She began to move quietly into the centre of the hall. With one hand, she held her cloak over her face; in the other, she held a strangely-shaped object. She drew near to the princess, who stopped dancing and stepped back, surprised.

'I have a birthday present for you, my lovely Aurora,'

said the old woman, holding out the strange object in her thin hand.

'Oh, thank you. But what is it?' laughed Aurora, as she looked curiously at it.

'You'll soon find out!' was the old woman's reply.

The musicians were still playing, so Aurora held her present over her head, and danced. The candlelight shone on it, as she spun happily across the hall.

'It's a spindle!' someone shouted.

'Give it to me at once!' commanded the king in sudden fear.

'Be careful, Aurora!' cried the frightened queen.

But it was too late.

'I've cut my finger,' said Aurora, and a drop of blood marked her silk dress.

Slowly, she fell to the floor.

'She's dead!'

'No! Oh, no!' cried the queen, running to her and kneeling beside her. 'No, she's not dead! She's sleeping.'

A dark shadow covered them. The queen looked up. The old woman stood over her. She let the cloak fall away from her face, and she smiled an evil smile.

'Carabosse!' the queen said, and she stretched her arms over Aurora to guard her.

Carabosse laughed, and the sound was ugly. She gathered her black cloak around her and disappeared in a dark cloud, as she had done sixteen years before. Again, the queen's tears fell on her sleeping daughter.

There was silence in the great hall. Nobody knew what to do. Then the candles began to shine more brightly, and the flowers to smell more sweetly. A soft sound was heard, and a gentle voice spoke.

'Take the princess to her bed.'

It was the Lilac Fairy. The four princes picked up the princess and gently carried her to her bed.

'How beautiful she looks!' they said sadly. They left her and returned to their own countries.

In the great hall, the Lilac Fairy waved her wand backwards and forwards, and drops of silver hung in the air. Everyone began to feel tired; they wanted to sleep; they closed their eyes; they slept. The fairy flew on shining wings through the palace, and everyone she passed fell asleep. She flew into the palace gardens.

'Let no danger come near,' she called, waving her wand in the soft evening light.

A forest of wild roses, the colour of Aurora's dress, grew over the gardens, all round the palace. It was too dark and thick for anyone to enter. Everywhere, people talked about the palace which had disappeared behind the strange and beautiful forest.

ACT TWO

The years went by, and the forest grew thicker and thicker, and the roses more and more beautiful. People forgot the story of the hidden palace.

One hundred years after the princess had fallen asleep, a prince was hunting near the forest.

'The dogs have run that way, my lord,' one of the huntsmen told him, pointing to a path which led away from the forest. 'We must follow!'

The prince, whose name was Florimund, did not answer for a minute. He looked up at the clear blue sky, and felt the sun warm his face. He heard the birds singing among the wild roses. The smell of the flowers was sweet and strong.

'I feel as if something strange is going to happen,' he said to himself.

He waved his hand at his friends and his servants. 'You go on. I don't want to hunt any more today.'

They left him, and he sat down on the soft green grass, with his head resting against a tree. He closed his eyes and soft colours shone in front of him. Then the lights danced away. He was asleep.

The colour of the roses became brighter, and they began to move as if blown by a gentle wind. The Lilac Fairy flew out of the forest. She waved her silver wand over the sleeping prince.

'You will dream of a sleeping beauty!' she cried.

Florimund moved a little in his sleep, and began to dream. In his dreams he saw a fairy, whose dress and wings were the colour of a pale flower, flying towards him. As one toe lightly touched the ground, she spoke:

'The Sleeping Beauty has been waiting for you for a long time.'

A beautiful girl walked towards him. He took her hand, and kissed it. Then they began to dance. In the dream, he could not feel the grass under his feet. He seemed to be flying and, as he moved through the air with the beautiful girl, music filled his head; it seemed to say to him:

'You're in love! You're in love!'

Suddenly, he was sitting on the grass in front of the tree again. He was awake, and the beautiful girl had gone. But the Lilac Fairy was still there.

'It wasn't a dream!' he cried. 'You're real! But where is the Sleeping Beauty?'

'I will show you,' the fairy promised him. 'Strike at the forest with your sword!'

As Florimund walked forward, sword in hand, the roses fell back, opening up a path through the forest. The fairy laughed for joy, and disappeared into the flowers. Then she appeared behind him, and then he heard her laugh in front of him. More and more in wonder, he drew near to the palace. He came to a huge gate. It

opened and he went through. A palace stood in front of him. Its doors opened, and the prince went in. He ran from room to room, and the Lilac Fairy danced in front of him.

'Everyone's asleep!' he cried, 'but where's the Sleeping Beauty?'

At last, the Lilac Fairy led him to the room where Aurora lay on her white silk bed, surrounded by roses. Florimund knelt beside her. He gently kissed her soft lips. She opened her eyes. She smiled at him, and held out her arms. They did not need to say 'I love you', because their eyes spoke the words. The prince took Aurora in his arms and they danced as they had danced in his dream.

Around them, all living things began to wake and stretch. The forest of wild roses disappeared as if it had never been.

ACT THREE

Hand in hand, Florimund and Aurora stood in front of the king and queen, who cried with joy when they saw their beautiful daughter again.

'He woke me with a kiss!' she told them.

'It's just as the Lilac Fairy promised!' they said.

They were both very happy when the princess said that she wanted to marry Florimund. He was as good and as kind as Aurora, and the king and the queen knew that he would bring great happiness to their people. They asked everyone—the seven fairies, the important people of their land, the rich and the poor—to come to the marriage of their daughter. The bells rang, the musicians played, and the people danced.

The Lilac Fairy waved her silver wand, and its magic light fell with her blessing on them all.

Petrouchka

Scene One
Rich and poor used to come from near and far to join in the fun of the Butter Week Fair. It always came to St Petersburg at the end of the long, cold Russian winter. It meant that spring was coming.

On the last day of the fair, St Petersburg was full of music, dancing and singing. The roofs of the tall houses were white with hard-set snow, and the round roofs of the churches shone like golden balls.

As night fell, hundreds of coloured lamps were lit in all the booths of the fair. Above the noise, the deep voice of the old Grandfather of the fair could be heard. He was telling stories.

In the centre of the fair stood a booth which had not yet opened to the public. Two little drummer boys, dressed in red and gold, walked up and down beating drums.

'Come and see! Come and see!' they cried. 'We are going to begin the most wonderful puppet show in the world. You have never seen puppets like these before. They are just like real people. Come and see!'

When a crowd had gathered in front of the booth, the drummer boys disappeared.

The curtains of the booth opened, and the old Puppet Master stood there. He wore a long cloak and a tall hat painted with coloured circles and stars. He looked like a magician.

'Good evening,' he said, as he bowed to the crowd. 'I have brought my puppets to dance for you. When I play my magic pipe, they will move like real people.

Here are my three favourite puppets, the beautiful

Ballerina, the Moor from Africa, and my dear Petrouchka,' the Puppet Master added, as he opened the curtains behind him.

On one side stood Petrouchka, a sad-looking boy in an old shirt and wide trousers. In the centre was the little Ballerina in a short white skirt. She had a rosy face and a bright smile painted on her lips. On her other side stood the Moor. He looked very proud and important in his rich silk clothes. He held in his hand an evil-looking sword, bright with jewels.

The puppets were standing still, but when the Puppet Master played his pipe, they began to dance. At first, each danced on its own wooden box. Then, suddenly, they stepped lightly off their boxes and danced across the floor.

'The old man's pipe must really be magic!' the people said to one another.

Petrouchka's dance was gentle and full of sadness. The people who were watching had tears in their eyes.

'He makes us feel that the world is full of sorrow,' they said.

They were glad to turn away and watch the little Ballerina. Her smile made them happy again. Her eyes seemed to ask them all to love her. Her little feet made small, quick movements as she spun across the floor.

'How beautiful! How perfect she is!' everyone cried.

The Moor held his sword above his head and sprang high into the air. His dark eyes were full of pride as he looked down at the people watching him.

'How tall and frightening he is! How proud he looks!' the people said to each other.

When the show was over, the Puppet Master decided to put each puppet into its own room, while he went off to have a drink with a friend.

'I can't understand what has happened to my poor Petrouchka lately,' he said to his friend, as they were walking along. 'He looks so miserable, and his clothes look so dusty and worn. It's as if he were tired of life and didn't care about anything.'

'You must be dreaming,' replied his friend. 'He's only a puppet!'

Scene Two

The Puppet Master did not understand that his three puppets had not only become life-like in their movements, but also in their feelings. Petrouchka and the Moor had both fallen in love with the little Ballerina. She was in love with the Moor.

In his simple room, Petrouchka sat dreaming about her.

'I know I'm poor and ugly,' he said to himself, 'and that I have no chance of winning her love. But I do wish she would be kind to me, and talk to me sometimes.'

He looked sadly round the room.

'It's like a prison!' he cried out. 'I want to get out!'

Like a bird beating its wings against the sides of its cage, Petrouchka threw himself against the door and the walls. But he could not break out. When he was too tired to try any more, he lay miserably on the floor.

As if by magic, the door suddenly opened. The pretty little Ballerina stepped quietly in.

'What an ugly room!' she thought. 'And what an ugly little person Petrouchka is! How dare he think that he's in love with me!'

She danced as lightly as a feather round him. She laughed to herself as she watched his sad face. But Petrouchka's unhappiness left him as he looked at her.

'Perhaps she does care for me,' he thought. 'Perhaps she loves me more than she loves the Moor! I'll show her that I can dance just as well as he can!'

He jumped up and began to dance. But he was so excited, and he danced so fast and jumped so high, that the little Ballerina was frightened. She ran quickly out of the room and locked the door. Poor Petrouchka felt his unhappiness return as fast as it had left him. He beat the walls of his room so hard that he made a hole big enough to climb through. But he was too miserable and too tired to escape. He lay down on the floor and watched his tears falling in the dust.

Scene Three

After she had left Petrouchka, the Ballerina decided to visit the Moor. She liked his room, because richly-coloured silks hung on the walls and bright cushions covered his bed. When she entered, the Moor was playing with a ball. He threw the ball very high and caught it in one hand to show her how clever he was.

'Petrouchka frightened me,' she told him.

'Don't waste your time with that silly boy!' said the Moor. 'Come and sit on my knee.'

He put his arms round her, and asked her if she would marry him. But, before she could say 'Yes', Petrouchka sprang into the room.

'I love you!' he cried to the Ballerina. 'You mustn't marry the Moor. You're too good for him!'

Petrouchka jumped up at the tall Moor and beat at him with his hands. But the Moor was strong, and Petrouchka could not hurt him. Suddenly, the Moor picked up his great sword. Petrouchka, seeing the shining metal, was afraid. He turned and ran into the fairground. The Moor followed him, waving his sword above his head.

Scene Four

Outside the booth, the fair was still full of noise and

movement. No one had heard the puppets fighting. But when Petrouchka ran from the booth, everyone stood still and stared. The Moor hurried after him, still waving his jewelled sword. Behind them ran the little Ballerina.

'Stop them! Please, somebody, stop them!' she cried, but no one moved.

Petrouchka had used up all his strength. He could not run any further. He fell to the ground. The Moor raised the sword high into the air. Then he struck Petrouchka with the sharp metal. He seized the Ballerina's hand, and disappeared with her into the dark night.

As Petrouchka lay dying, the Puppet Master arrived.

'What's happened?' he asked. 'Why is my Petrouchka lying on the ground?'

'He's been killed by the Moor!' someone told him.

'Send for the police!' someone else cried.

'He's run away with the Ballerina!'

Everyone was shouting at the Puppet Master.

'I don't understand you,' he said.

He picked up Petrouchka and held the puppet up for everyone to see.

'This is one of my dancing puppets. It's not a real person.'

'We've been dreaming!' they all said as they looked at Petrouchka. 'He's only a puppet!'

The old Puppet Master walked slowly back to his booth, pulling the torn body of Petrouchka behind him. When he reached the booth, he heard a loud cry of misery. Looking up, he saw a shadowy shape on the roof. It looked just like his Petrouchka! It was shouting at him angrily, and tears were falling from its eyes.

The Puppet Master was filled with fear. He threw the body of the puppet away from him, as if it were hot coals burning his hands. Then he walked slowly away. He did not dare to look behind him.

The Firebird

Scene One
In a palace in Russia long ago, there lived an evil magician, the Enchanter Kostchei. He had surrounded his palace and its gardens with a high wall, so that no one could get in or out. But even the Enchanter could not stop the birds from flying over the wall and sitting on the branches of his magic tree. Gold and silver fruit grew among the tree's dark green leaves. Underneath its thick roots, Kostchei had hidden a chest which contained an egg; in the egg was his evil soul.

One evening when the sun was setting, there was a noise like sails fighting against the wind. It was the beating of wings. Over the wall flew a bird whose feathers were the colours of the sunset. It was the Firebird.

It had been hunted all day by Prince Ivan and his friends. The tired and frightened bird thought that it would be safe in the tree inside the high wall. But the prince was young and strong. He climbed over the wall and quickly shot at the bird with his crossbow. His shot missed, but it made the Firebird fall from the branch and spin to the ground like a red and gold leaf. It quickly flew up again, but the prince jumped in the air, catching the Firebird in his arms. It struck at his face and beat him with its wings. Backwards and forwards they fought, while the fruit in the tree shone like cats' eyes in the dark garden.

The prince felt the bird weaken. Its round black eyes prayed for freedom, but the prince still held it prisoner. With a sudden movement, it pulled a brightly-coloured feather from its wing. It brushed it softly across Prince Ivan's face. He felt a strange warmth, and understood that the Firebird was giving him one of its magic feathers. Gently, he put the bird down. Stretching out its red and gold wings, it flew into the freedom of the night sky.

Alone under the strange tree, the prince felt afraid. The moon rose. In its silver light, he saw for the first time some heavy iron gates. They guarded the entrance to a wide path leading to Kostchei's palace.

As he stared through the gates, they opened. Thirteen girls danced into the garden. Each one wore a silver crown on her head. The most beautiful of the princesses ran to the tree, but she did not see Ivan standing in its shadow. He watched her, while she shook the tree until some of the wonderful fruit fell to the ground. The other princesses gathered it up and began to dance. They threw the fruit in the air like gold and silver balls.

Prince Ivan, his heart full of love for the beautiful princess who had shaken down the shining fruit, stepped out of the shadow of the tree. He threw a silver apple to her. She caught it. She stood still, surprised.

'Who are you? Why are you here?'

'I am Prince Ivan, Princess. I climbed over the wall after the Firebird. But who are you and why are you here?'

'The princesses and I are prisoners of the Enchanter. He keeps us in his palace all day. He allows us to dance in the garden in the darkness of the night. Sometimes the Firebird watches us from the tree.'

'Are there other prisoners in the palace?'

'Oh, yes,' she answered sadly. 'The magician has changed them into devils! And do you see those rocks over there?' she added, pointing. 'Once they were people, happy and free, until Kostchei changed them into stone with his evil power.'

'Can that power be destroyed?'

'Yes, but only with his death.'

'I must kill him!' said the prince.

'Kostchei has hidden his soul. He cannot die while his soul still lives,' replied the princess.

They stood in silence, watching the twelve girls dancing in the moonlight, until the princess said softly, 'You must go now, Prince, before the Enchanter catches you too, and changes you into stone.'

But Ivan only fell deeper in love with her.

'Let me stay,' he said, as he kissed her hand. 'Please, please let me stay and dance with you.'

Their hands touched; their eyes spoke of love. They danced until the moon disappeared into the pale daylight. Putting her arms around his neck, the princess kissed him. Then she turned and ran with the others through the open gates.

When Ivan tried to follow them, the gates crashed shut in his face. He shook them as hard as he could, but they would not open. As he stood with his face against the cold iron, he heard the loud noise of bells. The sky grew black. The gates flew open. He fell on the path at the feet of a crowd of devils.

Scene Two

Kostchei, the Enchanter, stood there. Behind him were the princesses, white-faced with fear. The devils threw themselves on the ground in front of their master. He looked down at Ivan. He raised his arms to the dark sky, calling out, 'May this prince be turned to stone!'

Ivan, looking at the princess, felt unafraid.

'Your evil cannot hurt me,' he told the Enchanter. 'But,' he thought, 'how cold and heavy my legs feel, and now my arms seem to be turning to stone!'

Then he remembered the Firebird.

'The magic feather will help me!'

With his cold, heavy fingers he pulled out the feather.

'The Firebird's magic is stronger than your evil power!' he shouted, holding the bright feather above his head.

The garden was filled with red and golden light. The Firebird flew over the Enchanter and his devils. He made them dance, and they could not stop. They danced and danced. When they grew tired, it would not let them rest. At last, all the devils fell to the ground in a deep sleep. Even the Enchanter weakened under the strength of the bird's magic. He lay down and closed his eyes. The Firebird took Ivan and the beautiful princess to the tree. It beat at the knotted roots with its wings. It looked at Ivan with its round black eyes as if it wanted to say,

'Help me, please help me.'

At last the prince understood. Looking closely at the grey roots of the tree, he saw something shining. It was a jewelled chest. He pulled it out and opened the lid. Inside was a large egg. With excited movements of its wings, the Firebird told Ivan to lift it out. It took the egg from him. It threw it into the air, caught it, and rolled it along the ground.

The Enchanter woke up. He moved slowly across the garden. His long fingers reached out towards the egg. But, as he touched it, Ivan lifted it high above his head. He threw it to the ground. It broke in half.

A great storm tore across the sky, taking the Enchanter's soul with it. Kostchei lay dead.

His death broke the power of evil. The devils

disappeared. In their place were happy, laughing people, who danced for joy. They brought a crown of jewels to Ivan. They knelt in front of him, shouting, 'Long live the king!'

Ivan stepped towards the princess and said, 'Will you marry me and be my queen?'

She put her hand in his, and replied solemnly, 'I will.'

They stood together, young and beautiful, in love and happiness. There was a gentle sound of wings, as the Firebird flew into the sky above them. They watched until the red and golden bird disappeared into the bright sunlight.

The Nutcracker

ACT ONE

It was Christmas Eve. The snow was falling in the quiet street outside the house of Councillor and Frau Stahlbaum. Inside the house, it was warm and noisy. Frau Stahlbaum was trying to get her family ready before her visitors arrived.

'Clara! Don't jump about when I'm brushing your hair!' she said to her youngest daughter.

'Go and wash your face!' she shouted at her son Fritz, but she smiled at Louise, her eldest daughter.

'How pretty she looks,' she thought. 'I'm sure that Hermann von Rattenstein will want to marry her.'

'Louise, my dear, bring me my jewel box,' she said, 'and help me to decide which earrings to wear.'

Her daughter picked up some shining rings from the box and gave them to her mother. As Frau Stahlbaum was putting them in her ears, Fritz ran towards her with a dead mouse in his hand.

'Go away!' she shouted.

'Oh! Throw it away!' cried his frightened sisters.

'Give it to me!' Fritz's father, Councillor Stahlbaum, walked angrily into the room. He seized the dead mouse and threw it into the fire.

'Oh, dear! Somebody's at the door,' cried Frau Stahlbaum, as the bell rang. 'I'm not ready!'

'Happy Christmas to you all!' called a happy voice, and into the room came Doctor Drosselmeyer, followed by his friend Karl. They were carrying a large chest, which they put carefully in the middle of the room.

'I didn't know you were coming this evening,' said Frau Stahlbaum coldly. She disliked the doctor.

'Why have they come tonight?' she asked herself angrily. 'I know he'll spoil everything! He's such a strange old man. The von Rattensteins won't like him.'

But everyone else was very pleased to see the doctor and his young friend. Karl was holding some Christmas roses.

'They're for you,' he said quietly, giving them to Louise.

'How beautiful they are!' she said, hiding her face in the flowers.

They looked at each other, and it seemed to them both that everyone else disappeared. They sat down together on a big chair, and Louise's eyes were smiling as she softly touched the roses Karl had given her.

'Louise!' her mother called, but she did not hear her. 'Louise!' she said again, and when Louise did not reply, she walked quickly over to the chair. She seized the flowers and threw them on the floor.

'Mother!' Louise cried, jumping up, but at that moment, the bell rang, and the room was soon full of laughing children. The bell rang more loudly. The von Rattensteins had arrived.

'How kind of you to visit us!' said Frau Stahlbaum, hurrying towards them. Her heart was beating fast with excitement, as she filled their glasses.

'Louise will be rich!' she thought, and she forgot that Louise was sitting with Karl again, and that her eyes were bright with love for him.

'Come, children!' called Doctor Drosselmeyer. 'Come and see what I have in my magic chest!'

He opened the chest with a large key, and began to take out pieces of coloured paper.

'Is that all?' asked Fritz, and the children looked sadly at the chest.

But the doctor put his hand deep down into the chest,

and pulled out something else. It was a beautiful fan from Spain; it was red and black, and opened and shut with a quick, exciting sound.

'It's for you,' said Doctor Drosselmeyer, giving it to a little girl with dark hair and large brown eyes.

'What's next?' he asked, as he put his hand back into the chest. He pulled out a hat; it was made of gold-coloured silk, and a bright jewel was pinned to the feather on the front.

'It's an Arabian prince's hat,' the doctor told them, as he put it on the head of a small boy at his side.

He pulled out two more hats. One was from China; the other from Russia. Then he pulled out some wooden soldiers painted in red and blue. Now all the children, except Clara, had a present.

'What's for me?' she asked, looking into the chest.

'Here it is,' the doctor replied, putting a large box of sweets into her hand, 'and I've something else for you!'

He held up a wooden doll with a large smiling mouth. He put a nut into its mouth, and pulled its legs. The nut broke in half.

'It's a Nutcracker Prince!' cried Clara in delight, taking the strange doll in her arms.

She danced round the room with it, showing it to everyone. As she danced past Hermann von Rattenstein, he took the doll from her.

'Give it back to me!' she cried, but he held it over her head and she could not reach it.

He laughed, as she jumped up and down in front of him. He pulled the doll's legs, pretending to break more nuts. One of the legs came off.

'You've broken it!' Clara cried out, and her eyes filled with angry tears.

Louise left Karl, and put her arms gently round her sister. She looked coldly at Hermann.

The doctor took the doll in his hands, and carefully began to fit the leg in place.

'There you are,' he said, giving the Nutcracker Prince back to Clara. 'What a silly thing to do!' he shouted at Hermann.

Hermann's face went dark red. He looked at the floor. His mother hurried over to him. His father followed her.

'How dare you speak roughly to my son!' she said to the doctor. 'We'll not stay in this house one minute longer!'

'Oh, please don't go! The evening's hardly begun!' cried Frau Stahlbaum. 'I'm sure that Doctor Drosselmeyer will say that he's sorry.'

The doctor turned his back, and the von Rattensteins walked quickly out of the house.

Frau Stahlbaum was very angry. She seized the box of sweets from Clara.

'You've eaten enough!' she shouted at her, and she put the box at the top of a tall cupboard.

'I think dinner is ready,' called Councillor Stahlbaum. He looked into his wife's angry face, and smiled at her. 'Come on, let's enjoy ourselves! It's Christmas Eve!'

Dinner was finished. Everyone had danced. The evening had come to an end.

'Goodbye, and a happy Christmas!' they called to each other.

The Stahlbaum family stood at the door and waved to their visitors, as they went out into the snow. Karl touched Louise's hand lightly, as he said goodbye. Then he too was gone.

'Off to bed, now,' said Frau Stahlbaum, giving the three children a kiss. They were all tired, and climbed the stairs slowly. But a few minutes later, both Louise and Clara returned.

'I forgot my Nutcracker Prince,' Clara said, picking it up, and sitting down in the big chair.

'And I've come to find Karl's roses,' her sister said, and she too sat down, with the flowers held to her lips.

'It was a lovely evening,' she added, smiling to herself.

They both fell asleep, and Clara began to dream about everything that had happened during the evening. The clock behind her struck midnight. Clara heard the sound, but in her dream the clock face was the face of Doctor Drosselmeyer. As the clock struck for the twelfth time, Clara dreamt that she was standing in the middle of the room looking at the fire, which shone red in the dark room. Suddenly, a large mouse—a mouse which was larger than her—jumped out of the fire.

'It looks like Hermann von Rattenstein!' Clara cried out in surprise.

She was even more surprised when more mice jumped out of the fire. It seemed that the first mouse was their king, and they were his soldiers.

The mice moved towards the chair where Louise lay sleeping.

'They're going to hurt her!' thought Clara, and her heart beat fast with fright.

'We'll save her!' a voice shouted, and a tall Nutcracker Prince marched quickly into the room, followed by his army.

'He looks like Karl!' Clara said to herself.

A battle began between the mice and the soldiers. Clara watched in fear as the Mouse King attacked the Nutcracker Prince. She took off her shoe and threw it at the mouse. But the mice were winning the battle. Some of the soldiers ran away. The Mouse King picked up Louise, and ran off with her. The Nutcracker Prince raised his sword in the air and followed them.

Clara stood in the middle of the room, and tears ran

down her face.

'Don't cry, my dear,' said Doctor Drosselmeyer, who now stood at her side. 'Dry your eyes, and I'll help you to find Louise and Karl. We'll go to the Land of Sweets!'

A ship sailed into the room. The doctor helped Clara to climb quickly on board, while the mice tried to pull her back. The ship began to move past the tall cupboard at the end of the room.

'I can reach my box of sweets now!' cried Clara happily.

The ship took them to a wonderful forest, where the trees waved their branches at them. Everything there was white and silver. Snow was falling gently, but Clara did not feel cold.

'Oh, look!' she said, as a beautiful girl danced towards her. She was dressed in white, and had a silver crown on her black hair.

'She's the Snow Queen,' the doctor told her, 'and these are her snow fairies.'

More girls, dressed in white, danced through the trees. They danced as lightly as the softly falling snow. They shone brighter and brighter, as they spun over the snow-covered forest. Clara closed her eyes, and the wonderful shining forest disappeared.

ACT TWO

When she opened her eyes again, she and Doctor Drosselmeyer were back on board the ship, sailing towards the Land of Sweets. When they reached the shore, the doctor helped her down. But she was not standing on sand or rocks. She was inside a huge box of sweets.

'It's like this box that you gave me last night!' Clara said in delight, and the doctor smiled.

'Let's sit down in one of these gold sweetpapers, and

watch,' he said.

'I've brought Clara to see you dance!' he called out.

Two dancers appeared in front of them. They came from Spain. They wore red and black clothes, and the girl carried a beautiful black and red fan. It opened and shut with the same exciting sound as the one Doctor Drosselmeyer had given to the little girl with the brown eyes. They danced, and the girl's red skirts made a sound as soft as a warm wind blowing through wild flowers. Then they moved faster and faster, and her skirts moved like the waves of the sea.

Clara was so excited that she could not speak. When the Spanish dancers had gone, three more dancers stood in front of her. Their skin was dark brown; their dark eyes shone as brightly as their silk cloaks. One of them wore a hat of gold silk; a feather and a jewel on the front of it made Clara remember the hat that the doctor had put on the head of the little boy.

'How exciting!' she cried out, as the dancers spun round the wonderful room.

As they danced away, six Chinese children ran in, all wearing hats like the one in the magic chest.

'How pretty they are!' said Clara softly, as she watched them dancing for her.

When they had gone, Clara thought that there would be no more dancing, but the sound of feet beating on the floor made her sit down again. Four Russian dancers, their knees bent, sprang into the room.

'How high they jump!' Clara said in wonder.

'Where are Louise and Karl?' she asked, turning to Doctor Drosselmeyer, as the Russian dance ended.

'We'll find them,' he replied, 'but first, you must watch the dance of the flowers.'

As he spoke, eight brightly-coloured flowers danced very quietly in front of them. They moved as if they were being blown by a soft wind in a sun-filled field.

'I must dance with them!' cried Clara, and she ran through the box of sweets to join them.

The flowers made a circle round her, while she danced. As she spun round, she saw two people dancing behind the flowers.

'Louise! Karl!' she cried out in joy. 'At last, we've found you!'

Karl danced with the two sisters in the ring of flowers. As they danced, all the people who had danced for Clara in the Land of Sweets joined them. Everywhere was full of music and colour.

'Wake up! Wake up! What are you two doing down here? It's nearly Christmas morning!'

Clara opened her eyes. Her mother was gently shaking her arm. Louise lay asleep beside her, Karl's roses still in her hand. She woke too, and smiled at her mother over the top of the flowers. Frau Stahlbaum kissed her. Clara was still holding the Nutcracker doll. She looked down at it.

'I'm glad that the Mouse King didn't hurt him,' she thought.

She put her arms round her mother's neck and kissed her.

'Oh, Mother! I've had such a wonderful time. You'll never believe me when I tell you where I've been in my dreams.'

The Nutcracker ballet sometimes has a fairy called The Sugar Plum Fairy. In this story Louise appears instead and dances to the fairy's music.

Giselle

ACT ONE

One summer morning in the village where Giselle lived, two men were quarrelling.

'My lord, you should remember that you have promised to marry the Lady Bathilde,' said one. 'You must forget Giselle.'

'Oh, Wilfred, how can I forget her?'

'You must, because she is only a simple village girl, and you are Count Albrecht, Lord of Silesia.'

'If Giselle knew that, she would be too frightened to speak to me. She believes that I come from a village too, and that my name is Loys. She has only seen me dressed like this.' The count pointed to his plain shirt and trousers. 'She doesn't know that I leave my cloak and sword in this cottage.'

'She'll find out one day,' warned Wilfred. 'You should put on your cloak, take your sword, and return to the the palace now.'

'Oh, leave me alone!' said Albrecht angrily. 'I must see Giselle. I can't live without her.'

Giselle had woken that morning feeling unhappy. She had dreamt that Loys was not a villager. In her dream, he wore fine clothes; and a beautiful lady, with a ring shining on her finger, stood at his side.

Albrecht went to her cottage. Giselle opened the door, but she would not look at him.

'My love, what has happened?' he asked.

She only shook her head.

'Giselle, I love you. You mustn't be sad,' he said gently, taking her in his arms.

They began to dance, and Giselle forgot her strange dream.

Watching them from the forest, was Hilarion. He was also in love with Giselle. His heart ached as he saw Giselle smile at Loys. He ran forward and threw himself on the ground in front of her.

'Giselle, Giselle! Love me, love me!' he cried.

Giselle stepped back, afraid. He tried to seize her, but Albrecht stood between them.

'Do not touch her!' he commanded, adding coldly, 'Leave us at once!'

'He speaks to me as if I were his servant,' thought Hilarion, and he looked at Loys curiously, before running back into the forest.

As he ran, the villagers passed him. They were on their way from the fields carrying baskets of fruit. When they reached the village, they began to dance because the harvest had been gathered and their work was finished. Soon Giselle joined them. She moved so gracefully that the others stood still and watched her.

'No one dances more beautifully than Giselle,' they said to one another.

A woman pushed her way through the crowd.

'Giselle!' she shouted angrily. 'Stop it at once! Do you want to die and dance with the Queen of the Wilis?'

'Oh, Mother!' laughed Giselle, 'I don't believe that old story. I dance because I love it more than anything else in the world.'

'Girls like you, who love dancing too much, die before they are married,' warned her mother, Berthe. 'They become evil spirits—Wilis. At night, they rise from their graves. Any man who sees them is in their power until sunrise. While it is still dark, they try to dance him to death!'

No one spoke. No one moved. They all felt afraid.

Then someone said, 'Let's have no more of these thoughts. We must prepare for the crowning of our

Harvest Queen.'

They all hurried away, glad to forget Berthe's strange story.

The sound of talking and laughing followed them, and into the village came the Duke of Courland and his daughter. She was the Lady Bathilde, whom Count Albrecht had promised to marry. They had been hunting with their friends in the forest. Wilfred was also with them. He had hoped to warn Albrecht, because he was afraid that the Lady Bathilde might see him.

The duke called, 'Wilfred, we are all hungry and thirsty. Can you find food and drink for us?'

Wilfred went to the door of the cottage where Berthe and Giselle lived.

'Will you prepare refreshment for the Duke of Courland and the Lady Bathilde?' he said.

Berthe brought out plates of bread and cheese, while Giselle filled the glasses.

The Lady Bathilde rested on a seat at the side of the cottage. She took a glass from Giselle in her long white fingers, and smiled as the sunlight shone on Albrecht's ring.

'Are you to be married too, my dear?' she asked Giselle.

'Oh, yes, my lady. I am to marry Loys.'

'I wish you happiness!'

As she spoke, the villagers, who were wearing their best clothes and had flowers in their hair, entered the village.

'It must be the end of the harvest,' said the Lady Bathilde.

'Yes, the last of the fruit has been gathered. Now everyone will dance and the Harvest Queen will be crowned,' Giselle told her.

'We will stay to watch.'

The villagers were surprised and pleased to see their

visitors. They bowed to the duke and his daughter. Then, joining hands, they began their harvest dance. When the dance was finished, four of the men walked over to Giselle and bowed to her.

They said solemnly, 'Giselle, we want you to be our Harvest Queen.'

Giselle smiled with delight, as one of the girls placed a crown of flowers on her head. Everyone danced round her. Giselle saw Loys behind the dancers and waved happily to him.

Suddenly, the door of one of the cottages opened, and Hilàrion appeared.

'Look!' he shouted, holding up a jewelled sword. 'I knew that Loys was not a villager like us!'

He pushed through the excited crowd until he was face to face with Albrecht.

'This sword is yours, my lord,' he said, bowing low, 'and you are Count Albrecht, Lord of Silesia!'

Giselle ran to them.

'Don't be so silly, Hilarion!' she laughed. 'He's not a lord. He's Loys!'

But, as she spoke, the Lady Bathilde came towards them.

'Why are you here, dressed like that, Albrecht?' she asked coldly.

He could not reply. She turned to Giselle.

'My dear girl, this gentleman, whom you call Loys, is Count Albrecht. I wear his ring,' she added, pointing to the jewel on her finger.

'It's not true! It's not true!' said Giselle, but then she remembered her dream.

Her eyes filled with tears. Very slowly, she began to dance, and her dance told the story of her love for Loys. She moved softly as a gentle wind, and smiled as she remembered her happiness. But, as she came near the end of her story, her dancing became wild and full of madness. First her mother, and then her friends, tried to stop her, but they were frightened by the strange look in her eyes. Giselle reached the end of her dance, and stopped in front of Albrecht.

'I shall kill myself!' she cried, pulling his sword from his hand.

'No! Giselle, no!' he shouted, seizing her arm and taking the sword from her. But it was too late. She had struck the sword into her heart.

They all watched, helpless with fear and sorrow, as she freed herself from Albrecht, and began to dance again. Her dancing became slower and slower, until she was too weak to move. She looked round wildly and saw her mother. She reached out her arms, but, as Berthe ran towards her, Giselle fell dead.

ACT TWO

Her body was placed in a grave in the forest near the path. The next evening, some of her friends passed by, and they looked sadly at the white cross shining in the darkness.

As they moved quietly on, Hilarion hurried to meet them, shouting, 'The Wilis are coming!'

Frightened, they ran towards the village.

A silver light filled the forest. Queen Myrtha and her Wilis, with their wings shining softly, had come for Giselle's spirit.

They moved towards her grave, calling quietly, 'Join us, Giselle, join us.'

They surrounded the grave and gently waved their white arms backwards and forwards, until Giselle appeared. Queen Myrtha took her hand, while the Wilis danced around them. Giselle too rose on her toes and moved softly over the grass. Then they all disappeared into the silent forest.

Albrecht, whose heart had been broken by Giselle's death, came that night with Wilfred to find her grave. Sadly, he knelt in front of the cross and placed flowers at its foot.

As the moon rose above the trees, Wilfred looked round fearfully and said, 'My lord, we must not stay here.'

'I can't leave her yet,' replied Albrecht.

'You must! It's not safe to stay.'

But Albrecht could think only of his love for Giselle.

'My lord, I can't stay in this strange place!'

'Then go, and I'll follow soon.'

At last, Albrecht stood up. But, as he turned to go, the Wilis appeared in front of him. He stood still in fear, and then he saw Giselle. He watched her as if she were in his dreams. Lightly, she moved round him, sometimes touching his hand, sometimes dancing with the other Wilis. Suddenly they were alone, dancing silently together in the cold moonlight.

The silence was broken by a frightened voice crying out, 'Let me go, let me go!'

Hilarion ran from the forest, followed by Queen Myrtha and her Wilis. They surrounded him. They forced him to dance. They drove him back into the forest, still dancing, until they came to a dark lake. He could not escape. He disappeared under the deep icy water.

Full of evil power, the Wilis returned for Albrecht. Myrtha pointed at Giselle.

'Dance him to his death!' she commanded.

Giselle was not yet completely under the queen's power, and she said quietly to Albrecht, 'Hold on to the

GISELLE

cross. It will keep you safe.'

He ran to the grave and put his arms round the shining cross.

'Dance, Giselle, dance,' the queen again commanded.

Giselle moved more gracefully than she had ever done when she was alive, because she was becoming a Wili. Her lovely movements made Albrecht leave the cross to dance with her. Their dancing was so beautiful that even the Wilis were full of wonder. Then Queen Myrtha told them all to dance.

The dancing went on and on. Albrecht felt himself becoming more and more tired. His eyes were closing. He wanted to die.

'The night is almost over,' Giselle told him. 'Be strong.'

But he was weakening. He was falling, and she could not hold him. But, as he fell, the sky shone softly. It was the sunrise, and he was safe. The Wilis had lost their power over him. They disappeared.

Giselle stood by the white cross, looking at Albrecht. He threw himself towards her and cried out, 'Giselle, Giselle, don't leave me!'

But she was gone, and he knew he had lost her for ever.

Historical notes

SWAN LAKE written by Begichev and Geltser based on a German legend
Composer Pyotr Ilyich Tchaikovsky
Original Choreography Marius Petipa and Lev Ivanov
First Performance Bolshoi Theatre, Moscow, Russia, 4th March, 1877

COPPELIA based on a story by E.T.A. Hoffmann
Composer Leo Delibes
Choreography Saint-Léon
First Performance Théâtre National de L'Opéra, Paris, France, 25th May, 1870

DAPHNIS AND CHLOE based on a Greek legend
Composer Maurice Ravel
Original Choreography Michael Fokine
First Performance Théâtre du Châtelet, Paris, France, 8th June, 1912

SLEEPING BEAUTY based on a story by Charles Perrault, based on legend
Composer Pyotr Ilyich Tchaikovsky
Choreography Marius Petipa
First Performance Maryinsky Theatre, St Petersburg, Russia, 15th January, 1890

PETROUCHKA written by Alexandre Benois, based on childhood memories
Composer Igor Stravinsky
Choreography Michael Fokine
First Performance
Diaghilev Ballet at the Théâtre du Châtelet, Paris, France, 13th June, 1911

THE FIREBIRD based on Russian fairytales
Composer Igor Stravinsky
Original Choreography Michael Fokine
First Performance Théâtre National de l'Opéra, Paris, France, 25th June, 1910

THE NUTCRACKER based on a story by E.T.A. Hoffmann
Composer Pyotr Ilyich Tchaikovsky
Choreography Lev Ivanov
First Performance
Maryinsky Theatre, St Petersburg, Russia, 18th December, 1892

GISELLE based on a Slavonic legend told by Heinrich Heine
Composer Adolphe Adam
Original Choreography Jean Coralli and Jules Perrot
First Performance Théâtre National de l'Opéra, Paris, France, 28th June, 1841

List of extra words

booth *a tent with one open side, used at markets or fairs*

cloak

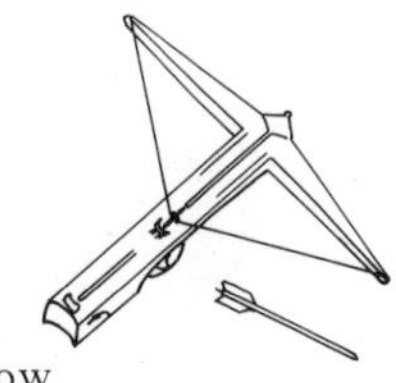

crossbow

doll

Eve *the day before (Christmas Day is December 25th—Christmas Eve is December 24th)*

fair *a gathering to which people come to buy or sell goods, and enjoy watching small shows*

fan

grave *a hole in the ground for the body of a dead person*

harvest *gathering of fruit or corn from the fields*

hunt *to look for and catch animals or birds*

ladder

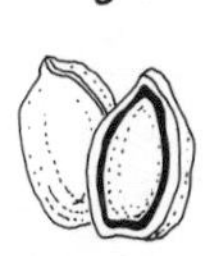

nut

pirate *a man who (with others) attacks ships at sea to steal their goods*

plaid *piece of check cloth*

puppet

root *the part of a tree or plant that is under the ground*

scene *part of an act in a ballet*

shawl

spell *words (or an action) with magic power*

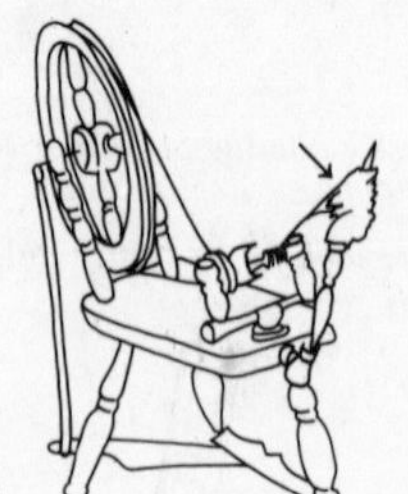

spindle

swan

wand *a magic stick*

Printed in Hong Kong by:
Yu Luen Offset Printing Factory Ltd